# A New True Book

# BACTERIA AND VIRUSES

## By Leslie Jean LeMaster

This "true book" was prepared under the direction of
William H. Wehrmacher, M.D. FACC, FACP
Clinical Professor of Medicine and
Adjunct Professor of Physiology
Loyola University Stritch School of Medicine
with the help of his granddaughter Cheryl Sabey

 CHILDRENS PRESS ™

CHICAGO

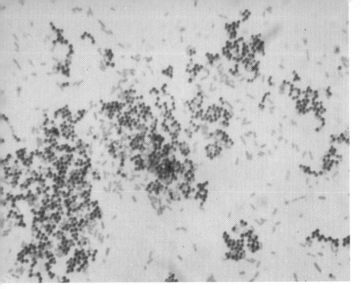

Some bacteria are shaped like rods.
Others are round.

Library of Congress Cataloging in Publication Data

LeMaster, Leslie Jean.
  Bacteria and viruses.

  (A New true book)
  Includes index.
  Summary: Explains good and bad germs, the different kinds, how they can help you, how some cause diseases, and how we fight diseases.
  1. Bacteria—Juvenile literature.  2. Viruses—Juvenile literature.  3. Immunity—Juvenile literature.  [1. Bacteria. 2. Viruses. 3. Diseases. 4. Health]  I. Title.
QR57.L46  1985        616'.01        84-27414
  ISBN 0-516-01937-6          AACR2

# TABLE OF CONTENTS

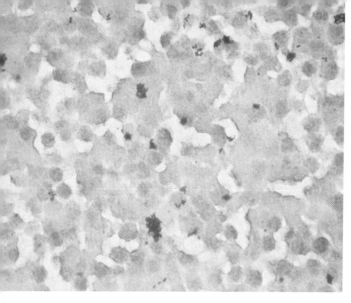

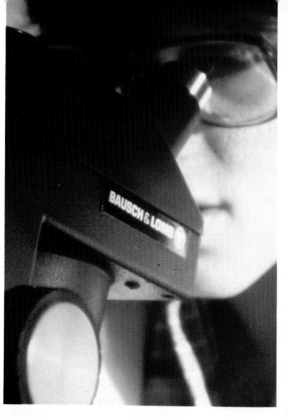

You need a microscope to see bacteria.
The bacteria causing pneumonia,
a lung disease, is shown below.
The type of bacteria that
causes boils and staph infections
is shown above.

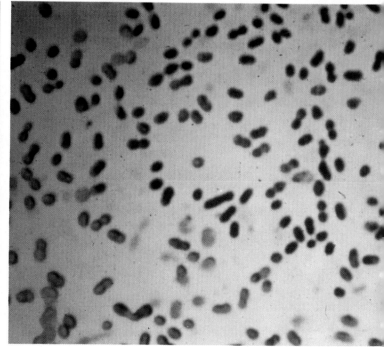

# GERMS ARE EVERYWHERE

We live in a world full of germs. Germs are everywhere—in the air, in food, on your body, and even inside your body.

Germs are tiny living things called microbes. They can be seen only by looking at them under a microscope.

Most germs are not harmful. They can even be useful. For example, many

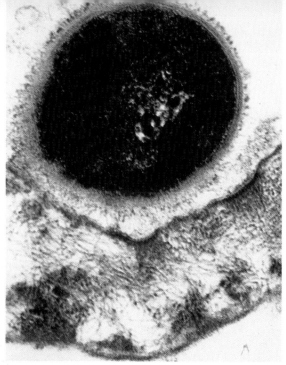

A cotton-tipped swab (top left) is used to place a bacteria sample on a petri dish. If conditions are right, the bacteria will multiply rapidly. The sample shown above left contains millions of bacteria. Under an electron microscope you can see the germs (right) used to make a vaccine to fight pneumonia.

germs can be used to make vaccines to protect people from getting certain diseases.

But some germs are harmful. They get into the

body where they can live and multiply. These germs can cause disease or infection (illness) in the body.

Some diseases can be contagious. This means that the germs can be passed from one person to another. Your body's own defenses will kill most of the bad germs that enter your body. But if the germs live and grow, they will cause an infection.

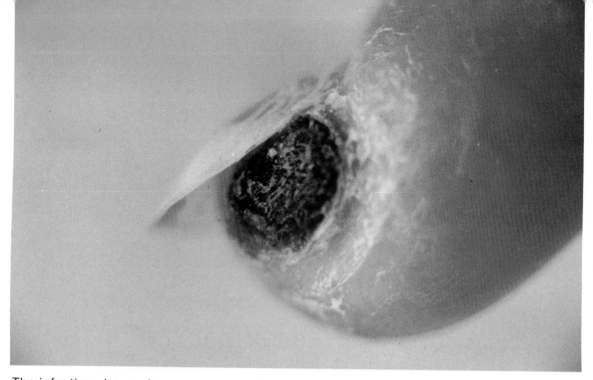

The infection shown above was caused by germs entering an open cut.
Below is a close-up of the staph bacteria that causes painful skin infections.

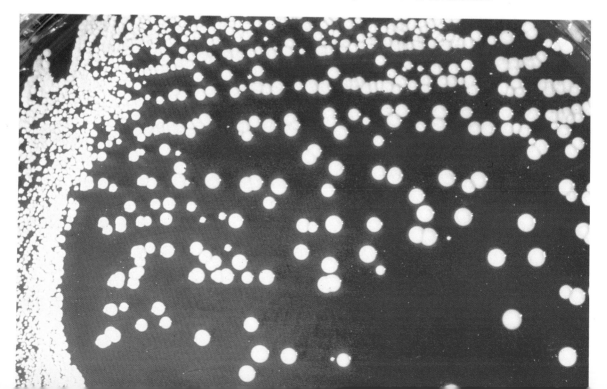

# HOW DO GERMS ENTER YOUR BODY?

Germs can enter your body in many ways. You can breathe in germs from the air. Germs can enter through an open cut or scrape on the skin. They may be carried by your blood to other parts of your body and cause infections there.

Mosquitos carry germs.

Germs can be swallowed with food or drinks. Flies and mosquitos can carry germs. They can pass the germs on by coming in contact with you or with the food you eat.

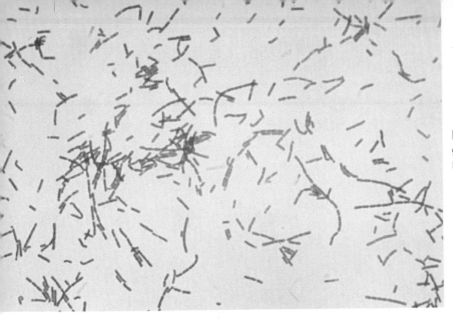

Rod-shaped bacteria growing in chains magnified 400 times

# WHAT ARE BACTERIA?

Bacteria are tiny one-celled germs that can be seen only under a microscope. There are many different kinds of bacteria. One kind is shaped like a short stick, or rod. Another kind is

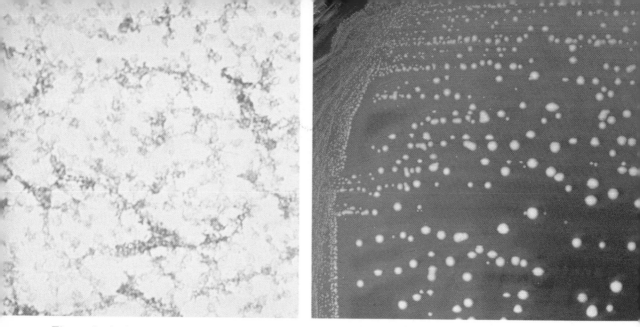

The spiral-shaped bacteria (left) can cause blood infections.
The round-shaped bacteria (right) can cause strep throat,
rheumatic fever, and kidney infections.

round. A third kind looks
like a spiral. They multiply
by splitting in half and
then group together with
their own kind.

Most bacteria are not
harmful, but some can
cause diseases, such as

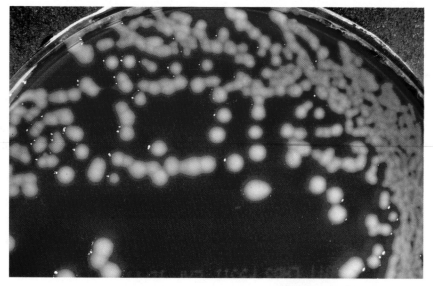

This bacteria can cause
a serious form of pneumonia.

pneumonia (infection of the lungs), strep throat (infection of the throat), some kinds of food poisoning (infection of the intestinal tract), and tetanus (infection of the nervous system). Medicines called antibiotics can kill bacteria.

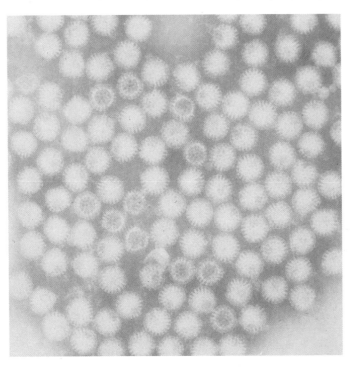

Sphere-shaped
virus

# WHAT ARE VIRUSES?

Viruses are one-celled germs that are much smaller than bacteria. They can be seen only under very powerful microscopes.

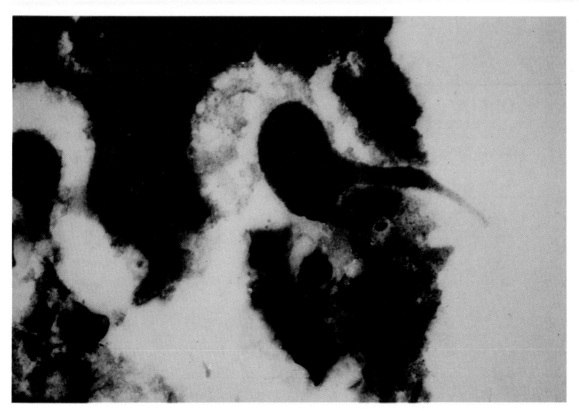
Tadpole-shaped virus

Some viruses are shaped
like spheres. Some are rod
shaped and have many
sides. Some look like
tadpoles. They can grow
and multiply only in living

cells. Many viruses are not harmful. If enough harmful viruses get inside your body cells and grow, you get sick.

Like bacteria, viruses can cause many diseases. Each kind of virus causes a different disease. Some viruses cause diseases of the skin, such as chicken pox and measles. Others cause diseases of nerve tissue, such as rabies and polio. And still other

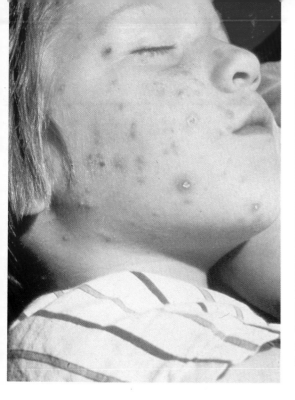

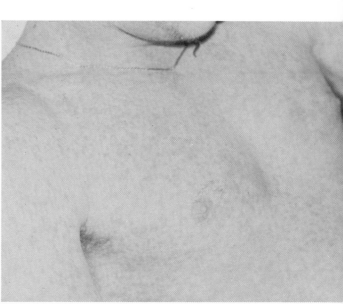

Measles (above) and chicken pox (left)
are caused by viruses.

viruses cause diseases of
body organs, such as the
flu and the common cold.

Few medicines can kill
viruses. Usually your body's
own germ killers will kill
viruses over a period of
time.

# WHAT ARE SYMPTOMS?

Symptoms are feelings that
tell you that something has
gone wrong in your body.
A fever, headache, sore
throat, cough, weakness,
aching, unusual tiredness,
and nausea are symptoms.

When your symptoms do not
tell the doctor enough about
what is wrong with you, he
or she will examine you.
The doctor will take your
temperature, look all over
your body, tap on your

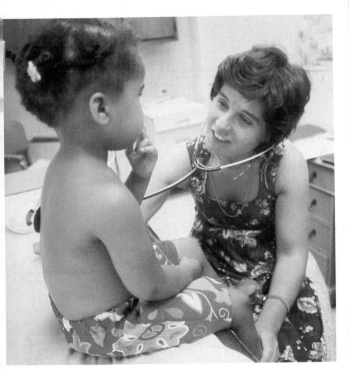

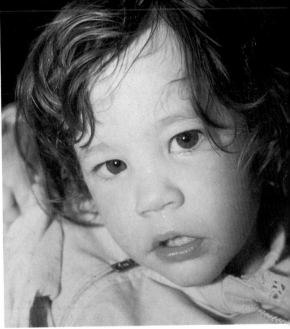

During checkups doctors examine you and look for disease. The little girl above has a cold. She has a runny nose and red eyes.

chest, and listen to your
heart and lungs with a
stethoscope. Sometimes, the
doctor must test your blood
or your urine before he
or she can be certain
how to treat you.

# WHAT IS IMMUNITY?

Immunity means being able to keep from getting an infection. One way your body becomes immune is by getting a disease and recovering from it. For example, once you have had measles, you will never get it again. Your blood's white cells fight measles by making germ killers called antibodies. The antibodies stay in your

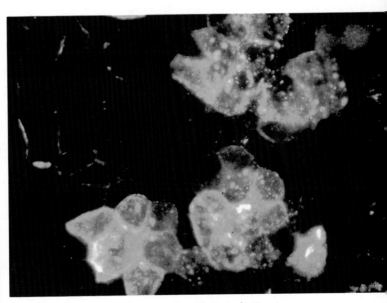

Close-up of the measles virus (above). Doctors have developed a vaccine that prevents measles.

blood and kill any further measles viruses that get into it, but will not kill other types of virus.

Another way to acquire immunity is by vaccination. A weakened form of a virus is injected into your

21

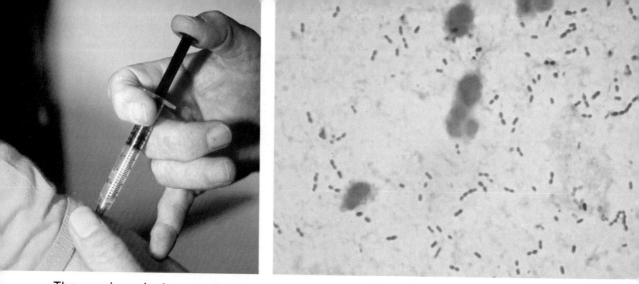

The vaccines doctors use to prevent or fight disease are often made from the virus that caused the disease in the first place. The virus used to make a pneumonia vaccine is shown at right.

body so that you get a very mild case of the disease. For example, if you are injected with a measles vaccine, your blood's white cells make antibodies to fight the virus. These antibodies protect you from getting measles again.

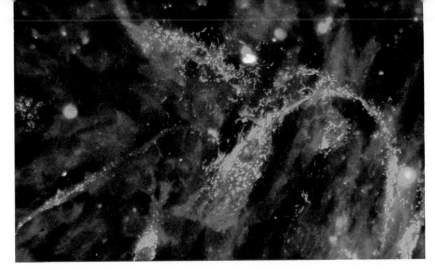

Microscopic view of a common cold virus

# WHY CAN YOU GET THE FLU MORE THAN ONCE?

Many different viruses can cause different kinds of flu. Before you get the flu, one of the viruses must grow inside your body. When you get the flu, your body makes antibodies to kill that

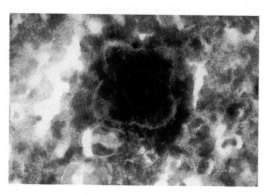

particular virus. The antibodies stay in your blood and keep killing that virus every time it enters your body. You won't get that kind of flu from that virus again. If a *different* flu virus enters your body, your blood will not have the right antibodies to kill the new virus. So you will get another kind of flu.

# WHAT IS A FEVER?

When you get sick, your body temperature may rise. That is a sign your body is trying to fight an infection. When your temperature is higher than normal, you are said to have a fever.

Normally, a part of your brain keeps your temperature around 98.6 degrees Fahrenheit. When

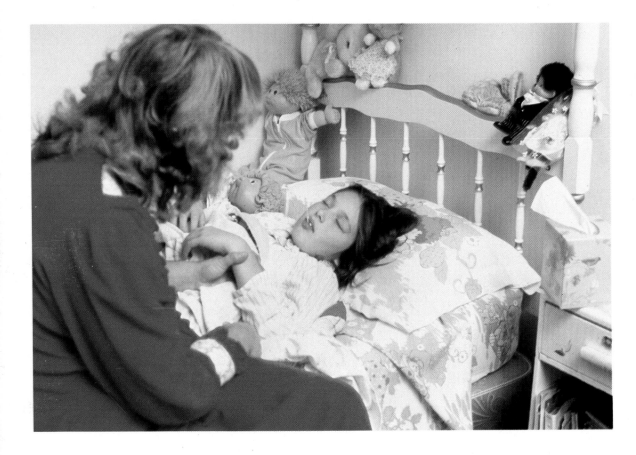

you get sick, a fever
makes your body produce
more chemicals and blood
cells to kill harmful germs
faster.

Ragweed (above) and
cat hair can cause
allergic reactions.

# WHAT ARE ALLERGIES?

Allergies are reactions of
your body to common
things it comes in contact
with, such as foods,
chemicals, animal hair,
pollen, dust, and drugs.

27

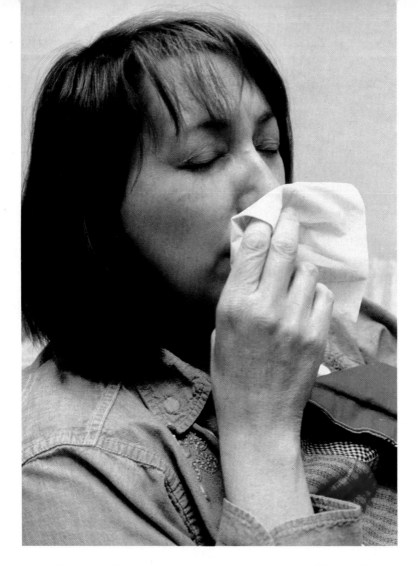

Allergies can cause itching,
sneezing, watery eyes,
runny nose, or even
breathing difficulty.

When something that you're allergic to (allergen) enters your body, certain cells in your body make antibodies. These antibodies join with the allergen and cause your body to release chemicals called histamines. They upset body functions and cause the allergy symptoms.

# WHAT MAKES FOOD SPOIL?

Food contains bacteria. The bacteria break down substances in food. Bacteria produce acids and gases in food that make the food harmful to eat. The longer bacteria grow in food, the faster food will spoil.

One way to prevent food from spoiling is to dry it.

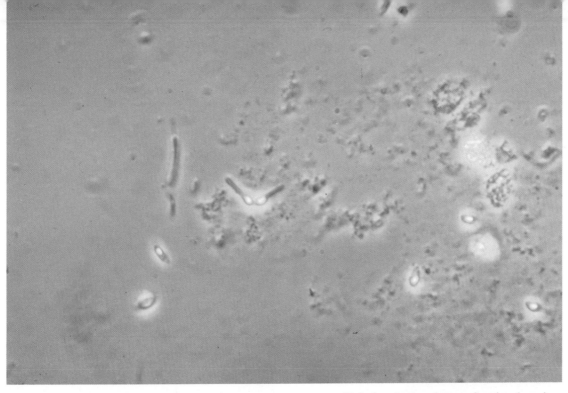
This bacteria causes food poisoning.

Bacteria cannot grow in food that does not contain moisture. Another way to prevent food from spoiling is to add salt to food, because salt keeps the bacteria from growing.

A common way to kill
bacteria is to cook food.
Heat kills bacteria.
Refrigerating many foods
will keep them fresh,
because bacteria cannot
grow in cold temperatures.

# MEDICINES

When bacteria make you sick, you may have to take medicine. Medicine may kill the germs or make them grow very slowly. It helps your body overpower the germs.

Long ago, many medicines were made from roots, vines, barks, and herbs. Today, medicines also come from plant, animal, and mineral products or from chemicals.

Medicine may be given orally (above),
in pill form (right), or by
injection (opposite page).

Medicine comes in
different forms. You can
take it orally (by mouth) in
the form of tablets,
capsules, or liquids. You
can inhale it in the form of
gases or sprays, or you
can take it in the form of

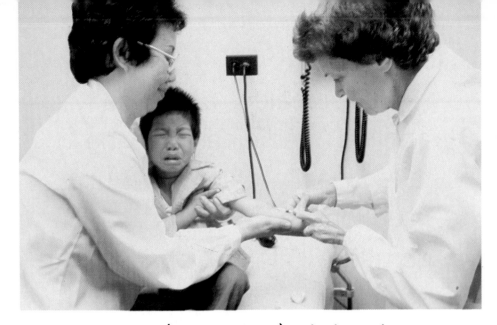

a shot (injection). Injections
are given under the skin or
into a muscle or into a
vein. Injections work faster
than pills or liquids.
Medicines also come as
solutions, creams, lotions,
and ointments to be
applied to an area on the
skin.

Oral, inhaled, and locally applied medicines can be taken easily at home. But injections have to be kept germfree (sterile) and usually are given only by a doctor or nurse.

# STAYING HEALTHY

It is not possible to
avoid all germs. But there
are ways to reduce the
number of germs with which
you come in contact.

Germs are everwhere. People fight disease-causing germs by keeping clean.

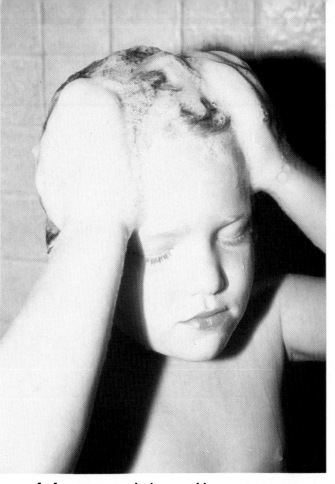

Many skin diseases can be prevented by keeping the skin clean. Bathe every day. Wash your hair regularly, and keep your nails clean.

Mouth bacteria can grow on bits of food and sugar remaining in the mouth, causing cavities and gum disease. Brush your teeth after every meal. Use dental floss to clean between your teeth.

Reduce the number of germs that enter your mouth by washing your hands before you touch or eat food. Don't use a friend's glass or silverware unless it has been washed. Stay away from anyone who is coughing and sneezing. You don't need someone else's germs; you have enough of your own!

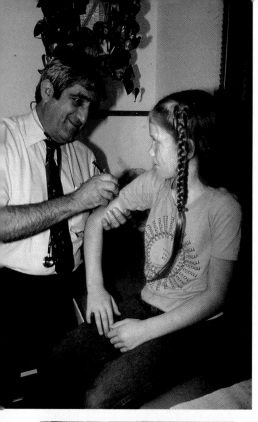

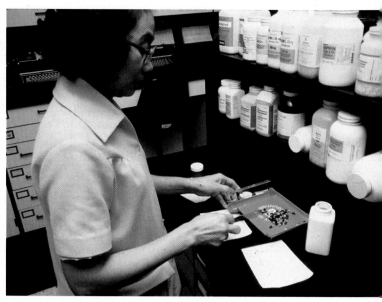

All medicines (below) must be manufactured
under germ-free conditions. They are
kept germ-free by protecting them with
glass or enclosing them in capsules.

Public health regulations provide safe water and milk to drink. Food control laws decrease chances of getting infections. Vaccinations that give immunity prevent many diseases. Antibiotic medicines are powerful destroyers of disease-causing germs.

Remember to take care of your body, and your body will take care of you!

# WORDS YOU SHOULD KNOW

**antibiotic** (an • ty • by • OT • ik) — a substance obtained from mold or bacteria that destroys germs or slows their growth

**bacteria** (back • TEAR • ree • ah) — one-celled living organisms that can be seen only under a microscope. The singular form of bacteria is bacterium.

**disease** (dis • EEZ) — a condition of illness due to disturbance of body processes

**flu** (FLOO) — common name for influenza, which is an infection of the breathing organs or intestines by viruses

**germ** (jurm) — a microbe or microorganism; a bacterium, a virus, or other microscopic forms of life

**immunity** (ih • MYOON • ih • tee) — protection from an infectious disease

**infection** (in • FEK • shun) — a harmful inflammatory condition caused by the entrance of disease-producing germs into body tissue

**inflammatory** (in • FLAM • ah • tor • ee) — an abnormal process in the body due to invasion by bacteria, viruses, chemicals, poisons, injuries, and other hurtful things. Inflammatory signs include redness, swelling, temperature increase, and pain

**injection** (in • JEK • shun) — a fluid that is forced into the body through a hollow needle

**microscope** (MY • kro • scop) — an instrument used to enlarge things that are too small to be seen by normal eyesight

**multiply** (MUL • tih • ply) — to grow in number or amount

**nausea** (NAWZ • ee • ah) — sick to the stomach a feeling that suggests that one may vomit

**pasteurized** (PAS • cher • ized) — heated to prevent or stop germs from growing in it

**reaction** (ree • ACK • shun) — a response to an influence

**solutions** (sol • LOO • shuns) — mixtures formed by dissolving substances together

**sphere** (SFEER) — round, ball-shaped object

**staph** (staf) — Staphylococcus, spherical bacteria that grow in clumps or clusters

**strep throat** (STREHP THROTE) — An inflammatory reaction in the throat produced by the streptoccus, spherical bacterium that grows in long chains like a string of pearls

**vaccination** (vac • sin • NAY • shun) — injection or inoculation of weakened or killed virus or bacterium to prevent the disease produced by the natural strong virus or bacterium

**vaccine** (vac • SEEN) — a fluid containing a weakened form of a particular virus, which is injected into the body to give immunity from disease caused by that virus

# INDEX

*About the Author*

*Leslie Jean LeMaster received a Bachelor of Arts Degree in Psychology and has taken postgraduate courses in clinical and physiological psychology. She has worked in the Child Guidance Clinic at Children's Hospital in northern California, helping parents and children with behavioral problems to interrelate. Ms. LeMaster has written other books in the New True Book series (Your Heart and Blood and Your Brain and Nervous System) published by Childrens Press. She currently owns and operates her own business in Irvine, California, and is the mother of a ten-year-old daughter.*